POWERED UP!
A STEM Approach to Energy Sources

# GEOTHERMAL ENERGY

## Harnessing the Power of Earth's Heat

MARIEL BARD

PowerKiDS
press.

New York

Published in 2018 by The Rosen Publishing Group, Inc.
29 East 21st Street, New York, NY 10010

First Edition

Editor: Melissa Raé Shofner
Book Design: Tanya Dellaccio

Photo Credits: Cover Arctic-Images/The Image Bank/Getty Images; p. 4 (left) Anton Petrus/Shutterstock.com; p. 4 (right) Perry Svensson/ Shutterstock.com; p. 5 Puripat Lertpunyaroj/Shutterstock.com; p. 7 (bottom) Kuryanovich Tatsiana/Shutterstock.com; p. 8 Matt Cardy/Getty Images News/Getty Images; p. 9 (top) Nikki Gensert/Shutterstock.com; p. 9 (middle) Semenov Victor/Shutterstock. com; p. 9 (bottom) Claudio Divizia/Shutterstock.com; p. 11 Linnas/Shutterstock.com; p. 12 (right) oriontrail/Shutterstock.com; p. 12 (left) JSvideos/Shutterstock.com; p. 13 ANNE-CHRISTINE POUJOULAT/AFP/Getty Images; p. 14 Designua/ Shutterstock.com; p. 15 (left) Daxiao Productions/Shutterstock.com; p. 15 (right) Bildagentur Zoonar GmbH/Shutterstock.com; p. 17 (top) Theodore Clutter/ Science Source/Getty Images; p. 17 (bottom) Jerry Dodrill/Aurora/Getty Images; p. 18 BERNARD MERIC/AFP/Getty Images; p. 19 (left) Paola Nerone/ Shutterstock.com; p. 19 (right) Adam Major/Shutterstock.com; p. 21 Evgeny Gorodetsky/Shutterstock.com; p. 22 Wisanu Boonrawd/Shutterstock.com.

Cataloging-in-Publication Data

Names: Bard, Mariel
Title: Geothermal energy: harnessing the power of Earth's heat / Mariel Bard.
Description: New York : PowerKids Press, 2018. | Series: Powered up! A STEM approach to energy sources | Includes index.
Identifiers: ISBN 9781538328514 (pbk.) | ISBN 9781508164289 (library bound) | ISBN 9781538328576 (6 pack)
Subjects: LCSH: Geothermal resources–Juvenile literature. | Power resources–Juvenile literature. | Geothermal engineering–Juvenile literature. | Clean energy industries–Juvenile literature.
Classification: LCC GB1199.5 B37 2018 | DDC 333.8′8–dc23

Manufactured in China

CPSIA Compliance Information: Batch #BW18PK For Further Information contact Rosen Publishing, New York, New York at 1-800-237-9932

# CONTENTS

# INTRODUCTION TO GEOTHERMAL HEAT

Earth is made of layers. People live on the outermost layer, called the crust. The innermost layers are the outer and inner cores, which are very, very hot. Heat moves out from the core and escapes through volcanoes, hot springs, geysers, and fumaroles on Earth's surface.

Heat from inside Earth is called geothermal energy. Today, we use about 7 percent of Earth's available geothermal energy to heat our homes and power our cities. Our use is sure to increase as **technology** improves and awareness grows.

FUMAROLES

AT GEYSERS, SUCH AS THIS ONE IN ICELAND, **PRESSURE** BUILDS UP AND HOT WATER IS PUSHED OUT OF THE EARTH WITH GREAT FORCE. SOME CAN SEND THOUSANDS OF GALLONS OF WATER INTO THE AIR IN A MATTER OF MINUTES!

## SUPERCHARGED!

Geysers are vents, or holes, in Earth's surface where water is pushed out by steam that has built up underground. Fumaroles are also holes in Earth's surface. However, fumaroles release, or let out, steam and other gases instead of water.

5

# EARTH'S LAYERS

The temperature just beneath Earth's surface stays between 45° and 75° Fahrenheit (7.2° and 23.9° Celsius). Under the crust is a layer called the mantle, which is made partly of solid rock and partly of hot, **plastic** rock that flows very, very slowly. Then there's the liquid outer core, which surrounds the solid inner core. Both core layers are made of iron and nickel.

Heat from the core warms the mantle. Underground water near the mantle may absorb, or take in, this heat. Geothermal energy comes from this heated underground water.

**SUPERCHARGED!**

Earth's crust isn't one solid piece. It's made up of numerous pieces called tectonic plates that drift away from or rub against each other. The places where plates touch are where many volcanoes form.

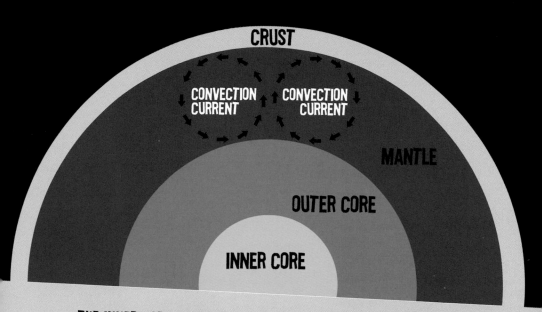

CRUST

CONVECTION CURRENT   CONVECTION CURRENT

MANTLE

OUTER CORE

INNER CORE

THE INNER CORE IS MORE THAN 10,000° FAHRENHEIT (5,537.8° CELSIUS). THAT'S AS HOT AS THE SUN'S SURFACE! **CONVECTION** CURRENTS IN THE MANTLE CARRY HEAT FROM THE CORE UP TO THE CRUST.

# HISTORY OF GEOTHERMAL ENERGY

Humans have been using Earth's heat for over 10,000 years. Long ago, people in North America used natural hot springs to keep warm and believed this water had healing powers. About 2,000 years ago, ancient Romans built bathhouses on top of the hot springs in modern-day Bath, England.

In 1904, the first geothermal power plant was built in Larderello, Italy. Its small **turbine** used steam to power five lightbulbs. Today, some countries, such as Iceland, use geothermal power as a major source of electricity.

BLUE LAGOON, ICELAND

BATH, ENGLAND

**SUPERCHARGED!**

Animals use geothermal energy, too! Japanese macaque monkeys enjoy taking dips in hot springs during the winter.

THE WATER TEMPERATURE OF THE HOT SPRINGS IN BATH, ENGLAND, IS ABOUT 115° FAHRENHEIT (46.1° CELSIUS).

# UNCOVERING HOT SPOTS

Sites that can supply geothermal power aren't always as easy to locate as other sources of energy, such as wind or the sun. Geothermal energy comes from deep underground, and most people have no idea there's so much energy beneath their feet. Steam, water, or **magma** need to travel all the way to Earth's surface to makes their presence known.

Geologists are scientists who study the earth. They look at maps, study **minerals** in water and soil, and dig deep wells to find geothermal hot spots.

## SUPERCHARGED!

Geologists aren't the only people interested in geothermal energy. Hydrologists are scientists who study water. Wildlife **biologists** make sure geothermal power plants don't bother nearby animals and plants.

GEOLOGISTS COLLECT SOIL TO CHECK FOR CERTAIN
MINERALS THAT MIGHT MEAN A HOT SPOT IS NEARBY.

# USING EARTH'S HEAT IN YOUR HOME

Heating and cooling a home with a geothermal system is different than using geothermal energy to create electricity. In home systems, long pipes are placed about 6 feet (1.8 m) underground, filled with water, and connected to the home.

In summer, the water in the pipes absorbs heat from the house. The heated water is moved outside, where it cools before returning inside. In winter, the ground stays warmer than the air, and the water in the pipes brings that warmth inside the house.

## SUPERCHARGED!

There are more than 600 hot springs in Iceland. Around 90 percent of the homes there are heated using geothermal energy.

HOT SPRINGS, ICELAND

 THIS IMAGE SHOWS A GEOTHERMAL HEATING AND COOLING SYSTEM USED IN A HOME. WATER FLOWS THROUGH THE PIPES, IN AND OUT OF THE HOUSE, TO CONTROL THE BUILDING'S TEMPERATURE.

# RENEWABILITY AND SUSTAINABILITY

Geothermal energy is considered a renewable resource because Earth's core produces so much heat that the amount people use is hardly noticeable. It's also considered sustainable, or able to last a long time. If used properly, reservoir water may be recycled back into the ground or immediately used again.

Renewable and sustainable energy sources are important. They provide us with the power we need without using up Earth's natural resources. They're also less harmful to the planet than nonrenewable energy sources, such as fossil fuels.

**SUPERCHARGED!**

Geyserville, California, actually has no geysers, but there are fumaroles and hot springs. Native Americans came to the area around 12,000 years ago and used the steam and hot water for cooking, bathing, and healing purposes.

TODAY, THERE ARE AROUND 20 GEOTHERMAL POWER PLANTS, SUCH AS THE ONES SHOWN HERE, IN GEYSERVILLE, CALIFORNIA.

# NEW TECHNOLOGY

Our planet has a lot of geothermal energy, but it isn't available just anywhere. Underground water is needed to bring Earth's heat to the surface.

Engineers are looking to create man-made underground water reservoirs as part of enhanced geothermal systems (EGS). In an EGS, water is pumped underground to create new reservoirs or refill empty ones. The hot rock around the reservoir heats the water. The hot water is then pumped up to the surface, where it's used to generate, or create, power.

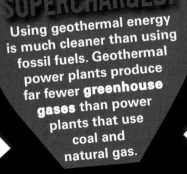

VOLCANIC CRATER, ICELAND

## SUPERCHARGED!

Using geothermal energy is much cleaner than using fossil fuels. Geothermal power plants produce far fewer **greenhouse gases** than power plants that use coal and natural gas.

ON AUGUST 12, 2016, THE ICELAND DEEP DRILLING PROJECT BEGAN DRILLING INTO A VOLCANO TO REACH A SPECIAL KIND OF STEAM THAT'S BEEN HEATED BY MAGMA. THIS STEAM COULD POWER ABOUT 50,000 HOMES WITH JUST ONE WELL.

# ENVIRONMENTAL CONCERNS

Geothermal energy isn't perfect. Engineers have to be careful about what minerals are in the water they're tapping into. Sometimes the water is high in **sulfur**, which can combine with oxygen in the air to create a gas called sulfur dioxide. Sulfur dioxide is bad for the environment.

Some newer methods of geothermal power production use high pressure to pump water underground to break through rock and reach reservoirs. This method is comparable to natural gas **fracking** and has been tied to seismic, or earthquake, activity.

**SUPERCHARGED!**

In 2006, an EGS project in Basel, Switzerland, was tested and put on hold after causing more than 13,500 small earthquake events! No one was hurt, but there was over $9 million in damage. The project was shut down completely in 2009.

THE CHAMPAGNE POOL IN NEW ZEALAND IS ABOUT 165° FAHRENHEIT (73.9° CELSIUS) AT THE SURFACE, WHICH IS A BIT TOO HOT FOR SWIMMING! THE WATER IS FULL OF SULFUR, WHICH GIVES THE POOL A YELLOW-GREEN COLOR AND FILLS THE AIR WITH A ROTTEN-EGG SMELL.

# OUR POWERFUL PLANET

Deep beneath the surface, Earth is hot and full of energy. People have used this natural energy source for thousands of years. Geothermal energy can be used to cook food, heat and cool homes, and power cities.

There are a few **environmental** concerns, but engineers are working to make geothermal energy a greater source of clean, renewable energy. It's a largely untapped resource that will be used more and more as we continue to learn about the natural power within our planet.

# GLOSSARY

**biologist:** A scientist who studies living things.

**convection:** The transfer of heat by a fluid from one place to another in a circular path.

**engineer:** Someone who uses math and science to do useful things, such as build machines.

**environmental:** Having to do with the natural world.

**fracking:** Pushing liquid, such as water, through the earth at high pressure to free up resources such as oil and natural gas.

**greenhouse gases:** Gases in the atmosphere that trap energy from the sun.

**magma:** Hot liquid rock underneath Earth's surface.

**mineral:** A natural element that is formed under the ground.

**plastic:** Able to be easily shaped or molded.

**pressure:** A force produced when something pushes against something else.

**sulfur:** A yellow chemical element that smells bad when burned.

**technology:** A method that uses science to solve problems and the tools used to solve those problems.

**turbine:** An engine with blades that are caused to spin by pressure from water, steam, or air.

# INDEX

# WEBSITES

Due to the changing nature of Internet links, PowerKids Press has developed an online list of websites related to the subject of this book. This site is updated regularly. Please use this link to access the list: www.powerkidslinks.com/pu/geo